DIESES BUCH GEHÖRT:

www.ingramcontent.com/pod-product-compliance
Lightning Source LLC
Chambersburg PA
CBHW021845170526
45157CB00007B/2940
* 9 7 8 1 0 7 4 7 9 3 3 4 0 *